IMAGES
of England

SMALL HEATH
AND SPARKBROOK

T0347020

IMAGES
of England

SMALL HEATH AND SPARKBROOK

Margaret D. Green

The
History
Press

Harry Johnson's van, advertising his business at 401 Bordesley Green, *c.* 1930.

Frontispiece: The new library in Green Lane, 1893.

First published 2002

Reprinted 2003
Reprinted in 2008, 2019 by The History Press

The History Press,
97 St George's Place, Cheltenham,
Gloucestershire, GL50 3QB
www.thehistorypress.co.uk

British Library Cataloguing in Publication Data.
A catalogue record for this book is available from the British Library.

ISBN 978 0 7524 2635 8
Typesetting and origination by
Tempus Publishing Limited.
Printed and bound in England by TJ International Ltd, Padstow, Cornwall.

Contents

Boys playing in a derelict terrace in Bolton Road, 1977.

Acknowledgements

All the photographs, except for those listed below, are from collections held by Birmingham Library Services and Birmingham City Archives.

I would like to thank the following for the use of their photographs: the Small Heath Local History Society for those on pages 13 (bottom), 25 (top), 27 (bottom), 54 (top), 56 (top and bottom), 59 (top), 60 (top), 61 (top), 65 (top and bottom), 80 (bottom), 83 (top), 85 (bottom), 86 (top and bottom), 87 (top and bottom), 88 (top), 90 (bottom), 95 (top); the Midlands Co-operative Society Ltd for 13 (top), 18 (bottom), 19 (top and bottom), 20 (top and bottom), 22 (bottom), 23 (top and bottom), 83 (bottom), 85 (top); Colin Simpson of the former Small Heath Harriers for 37 (top), 38 (top and bottom), 39 (top and bottom); and Jill Parry and Lynn Russell for 51 (top and bottom), 70 (top and bottom), 71 (top and bottom).

Also, a special thank-you to my sister Susan Abson for her help with the word processor.

Introduction

The name Small Heath first applied only to the area around the junction of Green Lane and the Coventry Road. It was within the Manor of Bordesley, which the new Borough of Birmingham acquired from the neighbouring Parish of Aston in 1838. Bordesley extended north to Garrison Farm, west to include Sparkbrook, and south-east to the River Cole. By the end of the nineteenth century, the whole district was known as Small Heath, excluding Sparkbrook, rather than Bordesley, and still covers two thirds of the ancient manor. The photographs in this book generally feature the period up to the 1970s, before the large-scale redevelopment took place.

In 1838 there were few settled areas in Bordesley manor. Industrial Birmingham was creeping in around Garrison Lane, with accompanying poor quality housing for factory workers. A small hamlet of mansions and cottages already existed in the Green Lane and Grange Road triangle. On the Coventry Road opposite Green Lane a tollgate stood until 1851. Local residents included many small manufacturers from Birmingham: gunmakers, brassfounders, buttonmakers, and a sword cutler, as well as several gentlemen, all attracted by the rural aspect of Small Heath. Some of the residences were quite superior. The belongings of the late Richard Harborne of Grange Road, when auctioned in 1840, included silver plate, china, pictures, books, fine linen, a grey carriage horse and a dairy cow. In nearby cottages were gardeners, labourers and wire workers from Horsfall's at Hay Mills. James Horsfall himself had a large house south of Grange Road. The wider district was largely open land with many scattered farms. The China Temple Fields still had a bowling green and tea gardens, and there were watercress gardens near Bordesley Hall.

The rural nature of Small Heath began to change from the 1860s. In 1862 the Birmingham Small Arms Company (BSA) built its new factory on open land at Golden Hillock, between the Birmingham to Warwick Canal and the Oxford to Birmingham Railway. The main owners of land were the Digbys of Elmdon Hall, and the Taylors of Moseley Hall, who also owned property in Sparkbrook. William Martin, architect and partner in the firm of Chamberlain & Martin, bought the Larches estate in Sparkbrook and the Regents Park and Whitmore estates. Resident at Whitmore House was John Lowe, a founder of the Birmingham cattle show. John Henry Chamberlain, architect of Highbury, the School of Art and the old Reference Library, lived at the Grange for fifteen years before building his own house in Edgbaston. As the wealthy drifted away, skilled and unskilled workers in large numbers were drawn in. Major brickworks at St Andrew's and Bordesley Green developed to meet the demands of local house building. By 1900 small manufacturing companies, timber merchants and masons spread eastward along Bordesley Green among the small shops and houses. Long straight uniform streets of tunnel-back houses were everywhere. Few open spaces remained, except at the northern and eastern boundaries.

By 1920, churches, billiard halls, pubs, picture houses and corner shops reflected the largely working class nature of the district. None of the old estates and houses remained, and the small professional class of residents clustered in the big houses around the park. Small Heath was now famous as the home of the BSA, Birmingham Football Club and the Harriers. Shopping on the Coventry Road was a big attraction too, with all the major chains and banks represented. In the 1930s attempts were made to remove the worst of the early nineteenth century slums around St Andrew's church, building the Holmes flats in Garrison Lane, and maisonettes at Kingston Hill. From 1925 the last of the farms along the River Cole at Heybarnes and Little Bromwich were acquired for municipal housing. During the Second World War, the mass production capabilities of companies like the BSA and Allday & Onions were vital to the war effort but attracted frequent and heavy raids by German bombers. Homeless residents drifted to the outer suburbs, a drift that continued after the war, adding to the neglect of Small Heath. Foreign competition in the manufacture of cars, bicycles, motorbikes, machinery and tools, for so long the main source of local employment, lead to its industrial decline. From the 1960s, Small Heath and Sparkbrook were the subject of many social and economic surveys and redevelopment plans. Settlers from the Caribbean and the Indian sub-continent have followed in the footsteps of earlier Irish immigrants.

Urban renewal and 'enveloping' schemes have preserved much of the late nineteenth century housing, but new houses have appeared around Little Green Lane, Grange Road and Bolton Road. Many residents lived for years near boarded up and vandalised properties, and vacant lots strewn with rubble, before seeing changes. Small community groups campaigned for the 'greening' of their terraces and for improvements to neglected local play areas. What little industry remains is small scale and scattered among several business and industrial parks. Local employment is mainly in retailing, with supermarkets at Hay Mills and St Andrew's, and in numerous family-owned shops. At Little Bromwich, the vast Heartlands Hospital has replaced the BSA as the largest single employer locally. The congestion of the Coventry Road can be avoided by using the Small Heath Highway, a new two-mile detour from Hay Mills to Watery Lane. The loss of the industrial heartland at Golden Hillock is clear; the railway line sees mainly commuter trains and the canal is a deserted backwater, leading to the Ackers Activity Centre.

In 1838 Sparkbrook was already separated from Small Heath by the canal, and later by the railway line alongside it. The Spark Brook, running from Stoney Lane to Walford Road, and joining the River Cole at Tyseley, was its southern boundary. It was settled in the late eighteenth century by leading non-conformists, including the Lloyds. Until the 1860s it continued to attract well-off middle class men to the big houses on the Stratford Road. However the existence of the BSA close by began to bring industry to the Sparkbrook side of the canal, and the BSA established proving grounds in the meadows of the Spark in the 1880s. There were soon coal and timber wharves and rolling mills on the south side of the canal, with a municipal refuse works in Montgomery Street. Since 1793, Birmingham had shipped its rubbish and night soil down the canal to Tyseley. At Sydenham Road, Alldays & Onions Pneumatic Engineering Company built a huge factory, near the Lion Nail Works. By 1914 housing for the working classes stretched as far south as Anderton Road. Sparkbrook, like Small Heath, was economically dependent on the industry around Golden Hillock, and declined in a similar way. It has remained a residential area with widespread redevelopment around Farm and Stoney Lane.

Margaret D. Green
June 2002

One

The Coventry Road

The railway bridge on the Coventry Road at Kingston Hill, 1948. The new St Andrew's football ground and Bordesley Urban Village dominate this view today.

Bordesley Hall, 1792. It was built in 1750 for John Taylor (d. 1775) a wealthy button and snuffbox maker and japanner, whose work was much admired by Dr Johnson. The house was burnt down during the Priestley Riots of 1791, was rebuilt and survived until the 1840s, where Dixon Road School now stands.

The Old Lodge public house at Bordesley Park Road, c. 1980. This 1930s building replaced an earlier tavern on the site of an entrance lodge to Bordesley Hall. It was demolished in 1986 as part of the redevelopment for Bordesley Circus.

The Coventry Road at Mount Pleasant, 1971. This elegant row of early ninteenth-century houses was due for demolition. Mount Pleasant marks the site of the drive to Bordesley Hall, which was set in thirty acres of grounds with a deer park and ornamental lake.

The view from Mount Pleasant to Sandy Lane and Watery Lane, c. 1914. Mitchells Bordesley Paper Mills, on the right, survived until about 1970. The adjacent houses were replaced in the 1930s by maisonettes.

The Coventry Road looking up to Kingston Hill, *c.* 1965. The Indian Workers Association was probably heading to Deritend to join a union demonstration, a familiar sight in the late 1960s.

New maisonettes at Kingston Hill, 1934. This small estate was built between the Coventry Road and Dart Street to replace some of the slum properties around St Andrew's church.

Boot repair shop at the corner of Herbert Road, *c.* 1910. These premises were the first Birmingham Co-operative Society shop in Small Heath, and opened in January 1882 to sell groceries. By 1886, when the road numbers were altered, and number 104 became 211, the Co-op had moved to a shop near the police station.

The junction at Cattell Road, *c.* 1935. The Greenway Arms was a landmark until wholesale demolition occurred here from the 1980s. From 1933, trolley buses, like the one on the right, replaced electric trams on the route to Yardley. The horse trough is now at Sarehole Mill. In 2002 a BigW superstore opened here.

Furnish complete at WALE'S

GREET

FURNITURE, CARPET & BEDDING WAREHOUSE,

131 & 132, COVENTRY ROAD, BIRMINGHAM.

FURNITURE FOR HIRE. Furniture Warehoused, Bought, or Repaired.

All Furniture and Bedding manufactured on the Premises,
and warranted substantial.

FOR GOOD AND CHEAP FURNITURE, GO TO WALE'S, who has the largest
Stock and cheapest, suitable for Drawing-room, Dining-room, Bed-room, or
Kitchen.

FOR GOOD AND CHEAP CARPETS, GO TO WALE'S, where you may buy
good Tapestry, from 1/11; good Brussels, from 2/11, and have them
properly made and fitted to your rooms.

FOR GOOD AND CHEAP BEDSTEADS, GO TO WALE'S. Full size Half-
Testers, from 15/- to 150/-; FRENCH, 7/6 to 50/-

FOR GOOD AND CHEAP MATTRESSES, GO TO WALE'S. Full size Spring
Mattresses, from 40/-; Full size Wool ditto, from 12/6

FOR GOOD AND CHEAP FEATHER BEDS, GO TO WALE'S, where you can
be suited from 40/- to 130/-; Flock and Wool ditto, from 6/6 to 30/-

Advert for Thomas Wales' furniture store, 1878. This grand shop was located opposite the
police station, but only survived a few years. Boots occupied half of the premises from 1908,
and can now just be seen in the photograph opposite, on the left.

14

The Coventry Road looking north to Herbert Road, *c.* 1910. Nothing shown here survives today. Small Heath Tavern, on the right, once famous for its pleasure grounds, was later renamed the Wrexham. A petrol station now stands where the Tavern once did, with new houses opposite.

Wimbush's bakery, on the corner of Little Green Lane, *c.* 1980. This famous local bakery was established in 1915 by Ambrose Wimbush, who sold cakes and sweets from a shop on the Coventry Road. A huge Morrisons supermarket now occupies the site.

The view north from Whitmore Road, *c.* 1900. The absence of traffic is in stark contrast to today.

The corner of Whitmore Road, *c.* 1970. Small shops still exist here. The road was named after the old house and estate, which had stood nearby since the eighteenth century.

Near Grange Road, c. 1910.

Near Grange Road, 1968. The new shops were built on land once occupied by Grange House, and later by the Grange cinema.

View towards Grange Road, with the cinema, *c.* 1930. This Co-op store was the first purpose built one in Birmingham, and opened in 1901. It was then the only building in Small Heath with electricity, supplied by its own generator.

The Birmingham Co-operative Society Ltd, 394-416 Coventry Road, *c.* 1941. It was damaged by bombing, losing the second floor meeting hall, but remained open for business with corrugated iron sheeting for windows instead of glass. The single-storey extensions were added about 1920.

Winter 1947. Although the Second World War was over, the people of Britain still suffered severe hardship at home, with food, fuel and clothing remaining on ration. Severe snowstorms and freezing temperatures in January and February added to the misery, stranding food and fuel supplies in docks and depots. In eighteen days one million tons of snow fell in Birmingham and by February over 60,000 industrial workers were laid off.

Small Heath Women's Co-operative Guild, 5 May 1930. Local guilds broadened the experience and education of their working class women members, inspiring some, like Edith Wills of Duddeston, to become councillors. These ladies were celebrating the 27th anniversary of their guild, with their president for the year, Mrs B. Rawes, wearing the chain of office. She was one of the few women to serve on the Co-op's general management committee.

The view south from Grange Road, 1968. The new shops on the left replaced the Co-op. The tower in the distance belongs to the old General Dispensary, built around 1895 by a charity that provided medical services to the poor.

Shops at the corner of Watts Road, c. 1929. The main Co-op shops, to the left of Mrs Allen's clothes shop, were remodelled in 1929, and the South Birmingham Furnishing Company was bought out to convert to a chemist's shop.

The new Co-op chemist's shop at Watts Road, *c.* 1930. All Co-op shops on the Coventry Road were designated Branch No 2, wherever they were, and however temporary. The generous opening offer was a free gift of Odol toothpaste or powder.

Interior of the chemist's shop, with fashionable Art Deco design floor and ceiling lights. Co-op shops aimed to give value for money, rather than a high-class shopping experience, with the added benefit of a bonus on purchases.

Looking north from Langley Road, 1890. The Coventry Road was still quiet, middle class and mostly residential.

Tornado damage at Charles Road, 15 June 1931. During the late afternoon of the previous day, Sunday 14 June, a tornado swept from Hall Green to Erdington, causing widespread damage in Small Heath to the shops and houses, and the park.

William Tay's butcher's shop, 574 Coventry Road, *c.* 1920. By the 1930s, dozens of famous retail names traded on the Coventry Road: Hawkins (drapers), Harrison, Johnson and Beckett (dry cleaners), Turner, Proffitt and Westwood (corn merchants), Caves and Jays (furnishings), Halfords (cycles). There were also photographic studios, piano teachers and pawnbrokers!

Advert for Wrenson's grocery shops, *c.* 1930. There were two branches on the Coventry Road, at 232 and 552. Other well-known grocers were George Mason, Pearks' Dairies, the Maypole Dairy and the Home and Colonial Stores.

The workshop of Clapshaw and Cleave, 598 Coventry Road, 1936. This well-known firm began making cricket bats in the early 1800s and moved to Small Heath about 1885.

Advert for the Whirlwind Skipping Rope, 1936, 'the last word in skipping ropes'. Clapshaw & Cleave made a wide range of athletic equipment from dumbbells to vaulting horses. The shop was in the city centre in Edmund Street.

The office, c. 1980. Beneath the black paint, the outline of the firm's name was still visible, and was once topped by a set of gilt wickets. The office was originally a tram waiting room when the service ran only to the park.

The Coventry Road near Hay Mills, looking north, c. 1930. The Singer car factory is on the left, with Little Hay farmhouse on the main road. The houses on the right still stand, now facing the Asda supermarket and a business park.

Hay Barn farm, 1925. It was still a working farm at this date, near the River Cole, but was soon to be developed for municipal housing as the Heybarnes estate. Nora Clift, who lived in the house then, attended Miss Florence Clarke's private school at 41 Golden Hillock Road.

Two

Sport and Leisure

Kingston Hill recreation ground, 27 June 1928. A visiting dignitary behaves badly at the opening ceremony.

Kingston Hill, *c.* 1995. Redevelopment plans in the 1980s marked the area for factory use but local opposition prevailed. It is now the only public space in Birmingham with a 'prehistoric' stone circle! It also has magnificent views of the city.

Dennis Howell (1923-98), MP for Small Heath from 1961 to 1992 and the first Minister for Sport. Born in Lozells, he was a Labour and union activist from a young age, but is more popularly remembered as a tireless crusader on sporting issues nationally and locally.

St Andrew's football ground, 1906. Birmingham City Football Club began in 1875 as Small Heath Alliance and had several homes until the St Andrew's ground opened on Boxing Day 1906. Play commenced only after thick snow had been cleared from the pitch.

Aerial view of the ground, 1926. Cattell Road runs along the bottom corner, lined with shops, and with courthouses behind. Tilton Road appears on the top right.

Football specials lined up in Garrison Lane, 24 September 1938.

GARRISON TAVERN,
GARRISON LANE.

Manager - - - MR. WILLIAM ARGYLE
(The football-followers' friend.)

Close to Ground.

Showell's ALES, ALWAYS IN FINE CONDITION.

"SHOWELL'S STINGO"
(Two years in cask).

A SURE REMEDY AGAINST CATCHING COLD AT FOOTBALL MATCHES.

Advert for the Garrison Tavern, 1906. A photograph of the tavern is on page 53. 'Stingo' was an eighteenth-century term for beer. Birmingham stingo was the subject of a ballad in 1763 and was praised as 'good humming liquor'.

The 1905 team. From left to right, back row: C. Simms (groundsman), W. Norman (trainer), J. Glover, A. Robinson, W. Adams (president), F. Stokes, H. Howard, J. Dougherty, Dr Stanley, Alf Jones (secretary). Front row: W.J. Beer, B. Green, A. Mounteney, W. Wigmore, W.H. Jones, F. Wilcox, C. Field.

The Cup Final team who lost against West Bromwich Albion in 1931. From left to right, back row: A. Knighton (manager), J. Crosbie, G. Morrall, H. Hibbs, A. Leslie, E. Curtis, A. Taylor (trainer). Front row: J. Cringan, G. Briggs, J. Bradford, E. Barkas, J. Firth, R. Gregg. Seated: G. Liddell, W. Horsman.

The Kingston cinema, c. 1960. Built in 1935, it is still a landmark feature on the Coventry Road.

The interior décor was in the Art Deco style of the 1930s, with seating for 1,400 people. It stopped showing films in 1968 and became a Ladbroke's bingo hall. It is currently used for religious meetings.

The Coronet cinema, c. 1935. Located on the south corner of Watts Road, it was built in 1922 and had its own orchestra giving concerts on Sundays for charity. It closed in 1963 and was demolished.

Advertisement for 'East is West' showing from 4 December 1922, promising 'laughter, tears, comedy, pathos, thrills and throbs' in seven reels.

The Ritz, Bordesley Green East, *c.* 1945. Built in 1927, it closed as a cinema in 1962 and continued for a time as a bingo hall, before demolition. The 1920s and '30s were the glory days of the picture house. In the inner suburbs they were almost as numerous as pubs.

The interior of the Ritz, 1928. Early cinemas were gloriously decorated, using rich colours like burgundy and gold. The style reflected the escapism, drama and romance of films in the 1920s and '30s.

Small Heath Harriers 1934-35, at the Bulls Head, Hay Mills. The Harriers began as Small Heath Athletic Club in 1891. A typical six mile run made a tour of Small Heath Park, continued through Hay Mills and over the fields, working back across Yardley, and returning via Green Lane.

The ladies section 1936-37, with their cups and medals for the season. Back row, left to right: C. Kendrick, B. Johnson, M. Pritchard, O. Lamsdale, C.Lewis (trainer and coach), H. Beeson, H. Wright, E. Anstey, M. Henn, P. Archer. Front row: D. Onions, V. Webb, V. Hemus, L. Pater, G. Tilley.

Colin Simpson at Salford Park, 1960. He joined the Harriers in 1944 and still runs with the Midland Veteran Athletic Club. Although best known for cross country and road races, the Harriers have always taken part in track competitions as well.

Cartoon by Norman Edwards celebrating the club's 1960 annual awards. He sketched local sporting events for the newspapers from the 1930s and is well known for his football cartoons.

The Harriers *c.* 1940, at the Three Horse Shoes, Sheldon. Four club members have taken part in the Olympics: Jack Price and Jack McKenna in the marathon in 1908 and 1924 respectively, Tom Collier in the relay in 1948 and David Black in the 5,000 metres in 1976 and in the marathon in1980.

The Harriers 1945-46. The club used many training grounds over the years, the Muntz Street 'celery trenches', Kingston Hill, St Andrew's and the BSA track. In 1980 it amalgamated with Solihull Athletic Club, preserving the name of Small Heath in amateur athletics, and gaining a permanent home.

The refreshment pavilion at Small Heath Park, 1914. The park was built on farm land donated by Louisa Ryland in 1876. Landscaping included carriage drives, ponds, shrubberies and flowerbeds.

Dredging the boating lake, 1937. It was probably undertaken because of the Coronation celebrations that year. The park's usual floodlighting was supplemented by 60ft high illuminated fountains.

Girls at the park, *c.* 1900. Louis Ryland would not allow games and music on Sundays, a restriction that continued until the Second World War. Sundays were for quiet walks and contemplation. The men lying on the grass must be contemplating the effects of Birmingham stingo!

The wild fowl pond, 1914.

The summer gala at the open-air swimming pool, c. 1925. The pool opened in 1883 on the Tennyson Road side of the park, and closed in 1938 as it did not meet new health standards! In 1955 a children's paddling pool was built on the site.

The winner of the water barrel race.

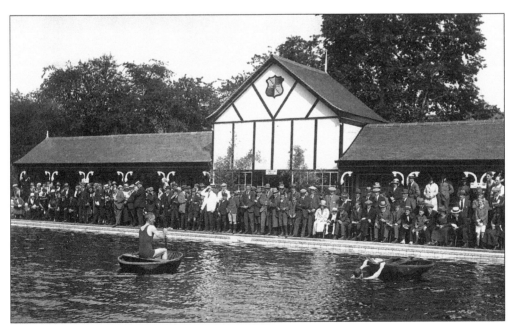

Coracle racing was not so easy.

Children paddling in the boating lake, 1916. Queen Victoria visited the park in 1887 and gave permission for it to be called Victoria Park, but local people preferred its original name.

A magician and assistants, c. 1950. The park has hosted concert parties, brass bands, dancing in marquees and fun fairs. In 1901 there were balloon ascents advertising Hudson's soaps.

Bonfire night, November 1972. The City's Parks Department began organising official bonfire and firework displays in 1961, hoping to reduce the number of bonfires in gardens, and accidents with fireworks.

A Punjabi band performing in the Pop-n-Jazz Festival, July 1971.

45

Hobmoor Ford in winter, *c.* 1920. The River Cole marks the eastern boundary of Small Heath for some four miles. This ford was a popular destination for summer walks and a favourite subject for local artists and photographers.

The Yardley Green crossing, *c.* 1925. In the river valley below, now Newbridge recreation ground, people came to picnic and play tennis and cricket.

Bertram Mill's circus at Heybarnes recreation ground, c. 1951. The open aspect of the River Cole from the Coventry Road north to Yardley has fortunately been preserved, the former meadows now grassland and tree plantations.

Circuses with animals are unacceptable today, but they used to be very popular and were well attended. A parade down the Coventry Road to the river was good publicity.

Demonstrating an experimental racing bike to Australian cyclists visiting the BSA sports ground, 1935. Local people were able to attend company sports days, military tattoos complete with brass bands, motorcycle acrobatic displays, dances and flower shows.

Young footballers with the Lord Mayor, Edward Hanson, at the old BSA ground, 1980. When the BSA closed, a large area of industrial land became available for reclamation. Pupils at Oldknow Road school suggested conservation and recreation areas between the canal and the Spark Brook, an idea which developed into the Ackers Activity Centre.

Three

St Andrew's to Bordesley Green

Clay pit south of St Andrew's Road, 1906, one of several in the area excavated for making bricks and tiles. This pit was filled in later and became the site of Kingston Hill recreation ground.

Lincoln Place, Garrison Lane in 1904, with the rear of Maxstoke Street on the right. Although Birmingham's worst slums were supposedly cleared by the 1880s, many on the fringes of the central district were left to deteriorate further.

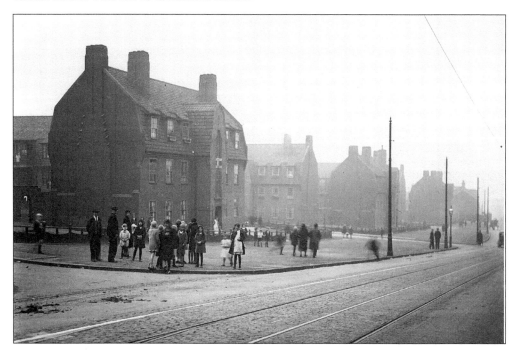

The Holmes flats, Garrison Lane, 1935. These were experimental flats built by the City Council to provide cheap accommodation, as many people could not afford the rents of the new council houses. Built in 1927, their good facilities meant rents had to be high, still excluding the poor.

The Harrison family of Sarah Street, *c.* 1905. Edward and Annie Harrison, with their children John and Lydia, had recently moved to the district. Their great granddaughters, featured on pages 70 and 71, were living in this same house in the 1960s, just before major redevelopment around St Andrew's church began.

Garrison Lane at Witton Street, c. 1975. Beyond the Garrison Tavern is the old board school, now a nursery and education centre. Callowfields recreation ground opposite, was created in 1910 on cleared slum land.

Five Ways, Bordesley Green, c. 1975. The Elite cinema stood on the corner of Crown Road, on the vacant lot next to the pool hall on the left.

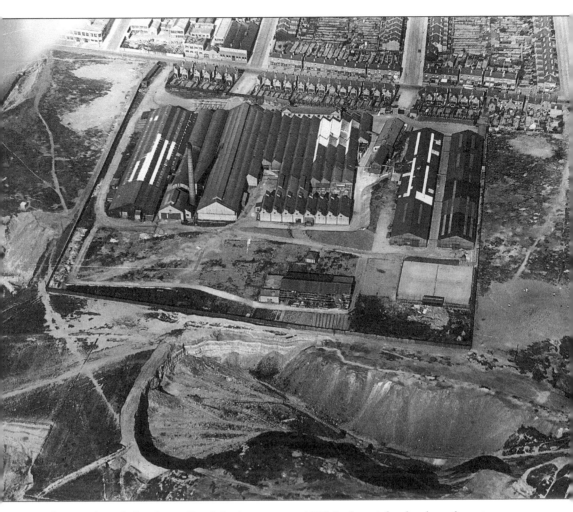

Aerial view of Bordesley Green Road, looking east, c. 1925. Left to right the three factories are: Terry & Terry's printing works; Hughes' cakes and biscuits bakery and Brocklebank & Richards' metal works. The roads opposite are, left to right, Burbidge, Cobham, with Thornley's varnish works on the corner, Ronald and Denbigh. The clay pit belongs to the Globe Brick and Tile Company, and is a good example of the vast size of some of these local pits.

Bordesely Green at the fire and police stations, *c.* 1910. The police station is still in use, but the fire station is now home to an engineering company.

Front view of the stations, *c.* 1910. After the formal opening of the fire station in 1907, the Chief Officer and the Lord Mayor were treated to a drive in the new motorised tender. However the driver lost control of the unreliable engine, and his very shaken passengers went home in horse cabs!

Bordesley Green looking south near Third Avenue, c. 1910. The lookout tower of the fire station, in the distance, was demolished in 1982. Shops here were family businesses, mainly grocers, newsagents and drapers. Many are now boarded up and out of use.

Near Blake Lane, 1928. Dallaway's garage is still there.

Herbert Powers in the doorway of his shop, on the north corner of Third Avenue, c. 1930. It is now a newsagents shop.

Bordesley Green, near Marchmont Road School, on the right, c. 1910. New houses in the side roads here were good quality tunnel-backs, with six rooms, and each house having its own outside lavatory, coal house and back garden. They attracted better-off working class people.

Bordesley Green and Belchers Lane junction, 1925. At this time Bordesley Green on the left, was extended right to become Bordesley Green East. This junction is now a major roundabout. The Broadway pub, now a McDonald's, was yet to be built at the top left corner.

View from the allotments at Churchill Road to the Post Office stores and factory in Fordrough Lane, c. 1970. The Post Office was a major employer for over fifty years but the buildings have now been demolished.

Bordesley Green East near the River Cole, 1932. Bordelsey Green was extended east to accommodate the new Batchelor's Farm housing estate, on the left.

Kenwood Road houses, Batchelor's Farm estate, 1926. After 1918, the government gave financial aid for municipal house building to help with the housing problem, but imposed conditions to prevent the building of long dreary roads of terrace houses. This design was inspired by the cottage-style at Bournville.

Yardley Green Road at Green Lane, c. 1890. Behind the hedge on the left is the Custard House, a farm estate dating back to the eighteenth century.

The Custard House Tavern, Blake Lane, 1962. Originally a private house built about 1853, it was bought by Atkinson's Brewery in 1888. Houses on either side were acquired later and incorporated when major alterations took place after this photo was taken.

View from Howlet's Farm, Little Bromwich, *c.* 1890. The farm was the site of the Infectious Diseases Hospital of 1895, built following the smallpox epidemic of 1893-94. It grew into the massive Heartlands Hospital of today.

Aerial view of the hospital, 1921. Yardley Green Road runs from the centre right towards the top left. Newbridge Farm is left of the allotments on the right, which now form part of the Yardley Green Leisure Gardens.

The Lodge of Yardley Green Sanatorium, *c.* 1910. Patients were kept isolated and their families could get little information. The names of the very sick might be posted at the gate: if a name disappeared, the patient was either deceased or recovered.

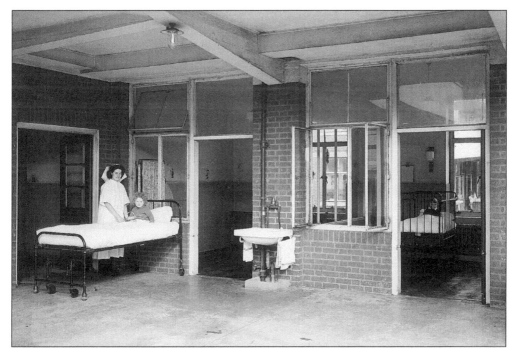

Children's open-air ward, *c.* 1930. The 'San' opened in 1901 to relieve its larger neighbour of smallpox cases, and became a tuberculosis hospital in 1910. Fresh air and rest were the only treatment until antibiotics and inoculation were developed in the 1950s.

Farm scene at Little Bromwich, 1888. The fields and farms shown on the aerial view on page 60 had disappeared under housing by 1939.

Bridge over the River Cole at Yardley Green Road, 1934. The road was called Newbridge Lane from 1810 when the road bridge replaced a ford and footbridge.

Four

Schools and Churches

Keep fit class at Somerville Road School, 1896.

Tilton Road School, 1972. Built in 1891, it was a typical Martin & Chamberlain board school, with a central hall and tower.

Wyndcliffe School, 1972. The brickwork has since been cleaned, showing its lovely terracotta decoration. It was built in 1878 as Little Green Lane School.

Girls at Little Green Lane School, 1910.

A mixed group of infants and juniors at Little Green Lane School, 1910.

Laying the foundation stone of St Oswald's church, 27 September 1892.

St Oswald's mission church, *c.* 1885. This opened in 1882 in a temporary iron building. The population of Small Heath was increasing so much that a number of iron churches and chapels appeared throughout the district.

St Oswald's church, c. 1920. Designed by W.H. Bidlake, it is an architecturally important church, completed in 1899, but no longer in use.

St Oswald's vicarage, Dora Road, 1954. Also designed by W.H. Bidlake, it is typical of his domestic work in the Arts and Crafts style. Both church and former vicarage are listed buildings.

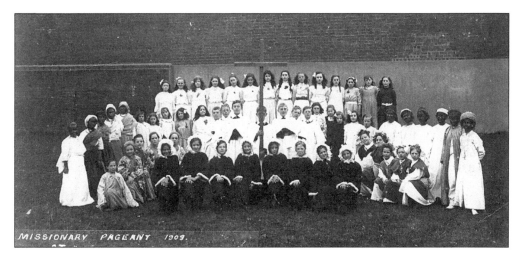

Children's pageant, 1909.

Carol service at St Andrew's church, 1949. The boys were pupils of St Andrew's School, Ada Road.

Opposite: St. Andrew's church, *c.* 1903. Completed in 1846, it was at first isolated among a few brick workers huts and cottages, before the population increased dramatically. It suffered storm damage in 1894 and the spire had to be demolished. The whole church was renovated from 1901, with practical support from the congregation, and the second spire lasted until about 1960. Redevelopment and declining attendance lead to closure in 1984, and demolition.

St Andrew's School, class of 1959. The pupil in the second row from the front, fourth from the left, is Jill Bradley, whose family had lived in Sarah Street since the early 1900s, and which features on page 51.

Class of 1964. In the middle row, third right of the teacher is Lynn Bradley, younger sister of Jill.

Recorder lesson, *c.* 1965. Jill Bradley is in the centre of the back row.

Class of 1969. Lynn Bradley is behind the teacher, on the right.

Baptist church, Coventry Road at Jenkins Street, 1891. The Sunday attendance in 1892 was recorded as averaging 800, and it was one of the leading Baptist churches in Birmingham.

Congregational church, Coventry Road near Muntz Street, 1912. It was built in 1868 when this part of the road was still residential. It features also on page 24. The church was demolished in the 1960s and replaced by shops.

Opposite: Wesleyan Methodist chapel, Coventry Road near Grange Road, *c.* 1880. Non-conformists were early settlers in Small Heath. The Wesleyans had their first chapel in Green Lane in 1841. This splendid building was erected 1876 while there were still open spaces roundabout. It is also featured on page 16.

Waverley Road School, 1972. It opened in 1892 with a bias towards industrial and commercial subjects. The building itself is a classic Birmingham board school, with a most impressive tower. The tower was partly practical for ventilation but was also meant to make a statement about the importance of education.

Boys French class, 1896. The average leaving age in 1910 was thirteen. The school became a grammar in 1945 and in 1965 moved to new buildings in Hobmoor Road as a comprehensive.

Boys Science class, 1896. Up to 1910, twelve schools were built in the district to cater for the growing population of children. Recently the reverse has occurred. Some schools have been demolished while Dixon Road School has been partly converted to flats.

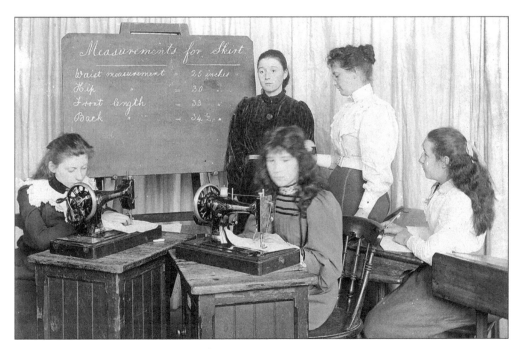

Girls needlework class, 1896. Girls were taught science but were not expected to make use of it, and the traditional domestic crafts were given equal emphasis. Waverley is currently a Sixth Form Technology College.

St Benedict's church, Hobmoor Road, *c.* 1920. This large red brick building in the Romanesque style was consecrated in 1910. The land for this church and St Oswald's was donated by the Digbys of Elmdon Hall.

Jenkins Street Conference Hall, 1894. Now in a poor state, this building was the inspiration of Joseph O'Dell, the well-known local evangelical Methodist. Originally used for worship, it has also been an annexe to Jenkins Street School and a community centre.

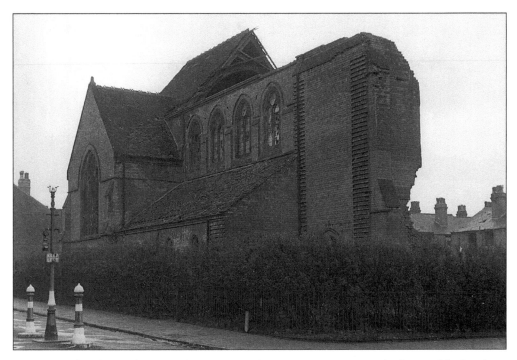

All Saints church, Cooksey Road, *c.* 1943. Built in 1875, it was severely damaged by bombing during the Second World War and was demolished. The area around has been completely redeveloped.

St Gregory the Great, Coventry Road, *c.* 1930. The construction of this Byzantine style church was begun in 1902 alongside the iron mission church of the Good Shepherd, on the right. St Gregory's closed about 1995.

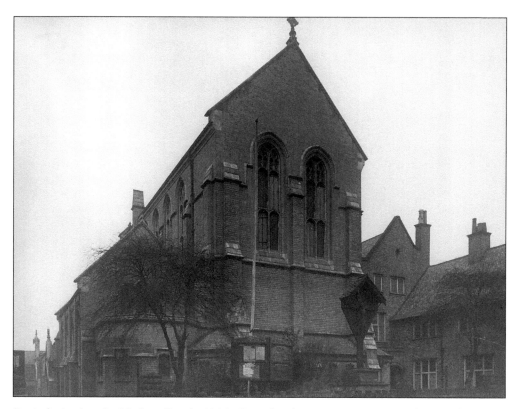

St Aidan's church, Herbert Road, 1946. Completed in 1898, it is a good example of the Birmingham red brick and terracotta style. The Anglican population of Small Heath has declined dramatically since the 1970s, and the church is now also host to the former parishes of St Oswald and St Gregory, and has been renamed All Saints. Cash from the sale of the closed churches supports projects at All Saints to help single parents, children, the elderly and mentally ill in the area, one of the most deprived in Birmingham.

Five

Green Lane to Six Ways

Beech Villa, Green Lane, c. 1980. When this delightful villa was built, about 1840, it was surrounded by open countryside. It is a surprising sight among the Victorian terrace houses as buses rumble past its gate.

Green Lane towards the Coventry Road, c. 1980. There are new houses on both sides of the road here, although the white villas on the left have been preserved. The block of flats in Arthur Street in the distance is the only high rise in Small Heath.

William Wright's newsagents shop, 539 Green Lane, at the Hobmoor Lane corner, 1916.

Green Lane in winter, 1895. The house is Green Lane Cottage, the home of Frederick Henshaw (1807-91), the landscape painter. Old Farm Garage, near First Avenue, now stands here.

Photographic portrait of Henshaw by Thomas Lewis, taken in the artist's studio, 1884. Henshaw lived in Green Lane for fifty years. The countryside around, and the lanes overhung with beech, oak, elm and chestnut trees, were his inspiration.

Green Lane in summer, 1894. The opposite view to the winter scene on the previous page, it shows the farm next to Henshaw's house. Both views were taken by Mr A. Brewster who lived in Green Lane.

Green Lane looking towards Hobmoor Lane, c. 1910. In the distance on the left, a decade before, stood Henshaw's house and the farm. The road is still a mixture of small shops and houses, but is congested with cars and buses.

The Vine Inn, 1904. This very old inn was demolished in 1927 and replaced by the large pub now called The Gables Tavern. About the same time, old cottages next to it were demolished to make a small road linking Victoria Street and Muntz Street.

Co-op shops, 549-555 Green Lane, c. 1960. On the corner with Hobmoor Road, they are now an electrical supplies store and fancy goods shop. The Co-op started up here during the First World War with a bread depot.

Burlington Road, c. 1900. This road is typical of the long lines of terrace houses, which obliterated the rural nature of the Green Lane area from the 1880s.

Street party in Bankes Road, celebrating the Jubilee of King George the Fifth, 6 May 1935. This, and other roads roundabout, Hugh, Somerville, Charles, Mansel, Flora, Kenelm and Dora, were named for the Digby family of Elmdon Hall, the largest landowner in the district in the nineteenth century.

Co-op shop, 252 Somerville Road, 1915. By 1914 there were fifty-seven Co-op shops throughout Birmingham, but many small retailers were unhappy about its success, believing the dividend was an unfair advantage.

Mr Cartwright selling groceries in Charles Road, 1934. It was still common for milk and coal to be delivered by horse and cart in the early 1950s.

Sale details for Monica Road houses
built by Charles Hougham, c. 1910.
They were for sale in blocks to private
landlords who would rent them out
for income.

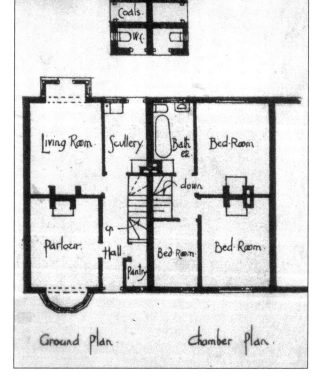

Ground plan of the finished houses
shown opposite. Few people owned
their own houses, even among
the middle class. Loss of income
through unemployment, illness or
the death of the breadwinner often
lead to eviction. These were nice
houses, with up to date facilities,
which was reflected in the rent.

Monica Road roughly marked the extent of private housing in this area by the First World War. From the 1920s, municipal developments filled the gap to the river.

Harry Rufus' grocery shop, 270 Monica Road, *c.* 1930. In the 1950s, it was run by his niece, Cath Judge, and her husband, but is now a house.

Arthur Street party celebrating the Coronation of King George VI and Queen Elizabeth, 1937.

Women protesters in Bolton Road, 1976. Almost the whole road was owned by a private company which had allowed the houses to fall into terrible disrepair. Described as the worst road in Birmingham, it was soon compulsorily purchased and the houses demolished, partly to make way for the Small Heath Highway.

Joseph and Lavinia Darrell, at Exeter Terrace, Bolton Road, c. 1925. Joseph had worked in the family's butcher shops since the age of twelve. With no welfare state to cushion their old age, he took casual labouring jobs until he died a few years later.

Many of the terrace houses in Small Heath had only a small dark yard, not a proper garden, but still attempts were made to brighten the area with a few plants.

Six Ways, 1958. Viewed from Waverley Road, Wordsworth Road is on the right, Glover Road ahead, Cooksey Road left, and Golden Hillock Road crosses left to right. A few yards left down Golden Hillock is now Poets Corner, a junction of the Small Heath Highway.

Mr McGee delivering milk in Waverley Road, 1910. Fresh milk from local farms was delivered daily to the door. Behind the fence is the park, with Tennyson Road at the rear.

Six

Transport and Industry

Cover of a Birmingham Small Arms Company trade catalogue for the Spanish market, *c.* 1920.

Small Heath railway bridge, 1907. A bridge over the canal and railway lines to join Small Heath and Sparkbrook was first suggested in 1884. It opened in 1904, providing alternative access to the bridge further south at Golden Hillock.

The bridge and new highway, 1984. Where the highway now runs were the Bordesley Junction marshalling yards, with twenty-seven lines. The tracks were laid in the 1880s giving access to the timber and coal wharves in Montgomery Street, Sparkbrook.

Small Heath and Sparkbrook railway station, *c.* 1955. It was opened in 1863 by the Great Western Railway to serve the new BSA works and the growing population in both districts. In the background is the south side of Byron Road, lost to the new highway.

Platforms and waiting rooms, *c.* 1920. Kings and queens on royal trains, and the rich and powerful from all over the world once alighted here to visit the BSA. Today it is a deserted commuter station.

Tram depot on the Coventry Road at Arthur Street, 1907. It was opened in 1905, with space to park ninety-four tramcars, when tram routes throughout Birmingham were being electrified. It was later used by trolley buses and buses, and closed in 1985.

Interior of the depot, 1907. Inspection pits were sunk between the rails for checking under carriages. Major maintenance was undertaken at nearby Kyotts Lake depot in Sparkbrook.

Drivers and conductors at the depot, *c.* 1910.

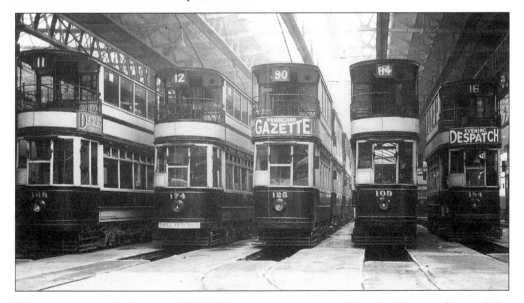

Electric trams at the depot, *c.* 1910. These cars were open only at the front and rear of the upper deck. Some cars remained completely open on top until the 1920s, giving passengers a cold ride in the winter.

Armoury Road with the new BSA buildings, *c.* 1920. The terraced houses in Armoury Road were built by the company for its key workers.

The First World War extensions from Golden Hillock Road, *c.* 1955. The car is in Armoury Road, and the Warwick canal is to the right. This block was built solely for the manufacture of munitions.

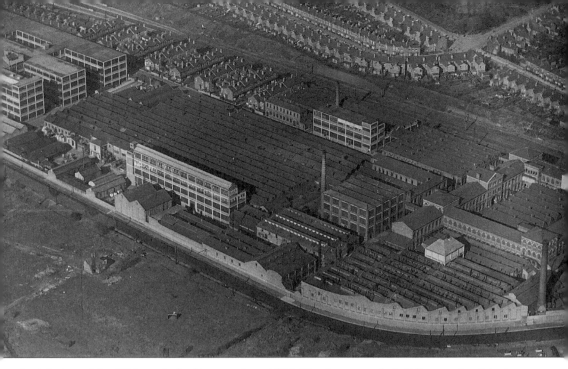

Aerial view of the BSA works looking north, c. 1930. The fortress style building on the right is the original factory of 1862. This photo shows how the works were tucked between the canal and railway line, with expansion space up to Golden Hillock Road.

Aerial view looking south, 1921. The Spark Brook flows from right to left, from the allotments to the Proof House shooting ranges. At the top is Seeleys Road at Greet, where Wilder's fire works factory also made use of the Spark's meadows.

The new building, 1915. During the Second World War, water was pumped from the canal to fight fires caused by German bombing. On the night of 19 November 1940, fifty-three workers were killed by a direct hit.

Workers in Golden Hillock Road leaving the BSA, 1914. The brick hut on the right features in the photo above, before the new building was erected behind it.

The barrel mill, c. 1916. The whole factory turned to armaments production in 1914, and the workforce rose from 3,500 to 13,000.

Testing Lewis machine guns, c. 1916. The BSA made every Lewis gun supplied to the British army in the First World War. Aware of the possibility of war, the BSA restarted armaments manufacture in 1936. Due to the threat of aerial bombing, production was eventually dispersed around fourteen factories in the area.

A cycle workshop in 1910. In 1878 the factory had closed for a year because of a total slump in the demand for arms. It reopened in 1879 to make bicycles and, by 1913, was the largest manufacturer of cycles and motorcycles in the country.

Men's canteen, c. 1914.

Motorcycle production, 1954. This model is the 650cc Lightning, a touring and racing bike previously made for export to America.

Packing cycle parts, c. 1955. The company had launched out into machine tools, cars and light engineering at the works in Waverley Road and Montgomery Street. By the 1960s it was in difficulties and was taken over by Norton Villiers in 1973. An industrial park now occupies the Golden Hillock site.

Allday & Onions Great Western Works, 1899. Located between Sydenham Road and the canal, it was an important manufacturer of forges, vices, steam-powered equipment and tools.

Trade catalogue of 1887 for the Spanish market, illustrating the use of mining equipment. It is easy now to underestimate the range and quantity of Birmingham products exported all over the world, from simple iron cauldrons to steam turbines.

Muntz Street factory, 1974. Small workshops or factories among the houses were a particular feature of industrial Birmingham in the nineteenth century. This one was located between Wright Street and Hawkes Street.

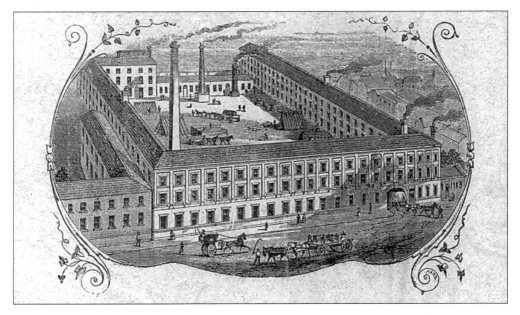

Royal Machine Works, Herbert Road and Jenkins Street, c. 1885. A few small factories were built here, parts of which are still in use. The Machine Works made cycles, and next door the Regent Works made hooks and eyes, and the Canada Works made revolving shutters.

Aerial view of Coventry Road factories, 1926. Oldknow Road is left, with the Roman Catholic Holy Family church, school and manse on the corner of the main road. The Singer Company began making cars here in 1927 in the BSA buildings.

Rear of the factories from the canal, c. 1980. From 1966 the Singer factory was used by Rootes and other companies for making components before being demolished in the late 1980s.

Singer workers making wooden car frames, 1931. Bernard Avern-Carr, by the window, was an experienced woodworker, having been taught by his father, a wheelwright.

The workforce in 1930. The Singer became one of the leading car manufacturers in this country, but fierce foreign competition in the 1950s lead to its closure in 1965.

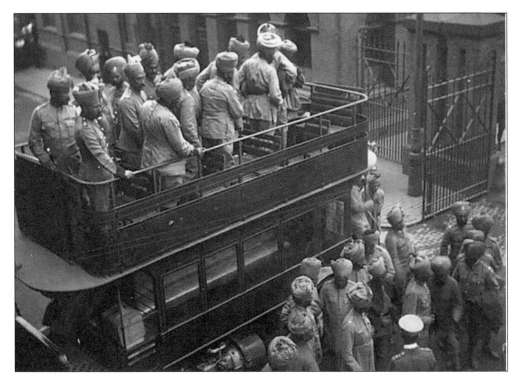

An Indian regiment visiting the BSA, 16 June 1911. About forty men toured the factory before travelling on to Warwick Castle. The visit was probably organised as a day out before they took part in the coronation procession of George IV on 22 June.

Shah Nasir al-Din progressing through Small Heath, 11 July 1889. The visit to Birmingham was arranged to try to impress him with western industrial power and extend British influence in Iran. However he spent only a short time at the BSA, and was more impressed by Osler's glass factory. The unfortunate man was assassinated in 1896.

Seven

Sparkbrook: the Stratford Road

An old painting of the tollgate on the Statford Road at the junction with Ladypool Lane, *c.* 1830. In 1851, tollgates at the Birmingham boundary were removed because they caused traffic congestion.

The Stratford Road from Kyotts Lake Road, looking back to Camp Hill railway bridge, *c.* 1910.

A horse bus travelling south from the city, with shops at Main Road in the distance, 1912.

The Stratford Road looking south at Farm Road, *c.* 1880. Strangely quiet, the only sign of life is the carrier's wagon in the distance. Christ Church School is on the right.

The same view twenty-five years later, in 1905. Steam trams, like the one shown, had run down to Sparkhill since around 1885. New track is being laid for electric trams, introduced throughout Birmingham from about 1906.

Christ Church School, 1949. The school first opened in 1867 in a private house and transferred to the new building in 1871, with places for 565 children.

Afternoon games lesson, 1949.

The temporary Municipal Bank, 163 Stratford Road, 1919. A bank backed by the city authorities was the idea of Neville Chamberlain during the First World War. It encouraged self-help and thrift, and soon found favour with the working classes. This branch was remodelled in 1921 into the trademark style to be seen in every suburban shopping centre.

The Stratford Road junction with Ladypool Lane, c. 1955. These premises had previously been a greengrocers and drapers.

The old Post Office next to the Angel Inn, *c.* 1880. From about 1890 to 1915, the sub-postmaster was William Henry Coe, who supplemented his income by selling books, and then boots and shoes.

The Angel Inn, *c.* 1870. Built in the eighteenth century, when the Stratford Road was a country Lane, most of the customers then were travellers forced to stop at the tollgate next door.

112

The Stratford Road near Stoney Lane, looking south, 1873. The land on the left belonged to the Poplars, the home for many years of Thomas Simcox, a Birmingham lawyer. Just beyond, the Spark Brook flows beneath the road. By 1890 houses filled the right side, and by 1918, the Poplars estate, Abbottsford and Hind's farm were lost beneath Conway Road Schools and the Empire skating rink.

St Agatha's church, *c.* 1910. Consecrated in 1901, it was built with money raised from the sale of Christ Church in Victoria Square. The architect was W.H. Bidlake, and this church is considered to be one of his best. It has many Arts and Crafts features, which have lead it becoming a listed building. The tower suffered bomb damage during the Second World War, and in 1957, Bidlake's furnishings were unfortunately destroyed by fire.

Aerial view taken from the scaffolding on St Agatha's church, probably during construction, c. 1900. The road running left to right is the south end of Gladstone Road, with neat rear gardens.

The north end of Gladstone Road, with Grantham Road and Christ Church. The chimneys in the distance belong to factories near Anderton Road, alongside the canal and railway line at Small Heath.

View down the Stratford Road from St Agatha's church. The waste ground on the left is the undeveloped end of Walford Road. On the right is the area around Stoney Lane. The section of road beyond the Baptist church is the same as that shown on page 113.

View north from the Sparkbrook boundary c. 1900. On the left at the Diamond Jubilee Store, is the corner of Stoney Lane.

Eight

Sparkbrook: Side Roads

Rioters destroying Fair Hill, the home of Joseph Priestley, 14 July 1791. Two thousand men looted and burned the house, regarding Priestley as the leader of anti-church and government sentiment inspired by the French Revolution.

Old houses in Farm Road, 1895. To the left of Thomas Smith's flower shop and nursery lived Lister Long, manufacturer of umbrella fittings.

The rear of the Limes and the Myrtles, terrace houses in Dearman Road, seen from a bombed site in Montgomery Street, 1949. The outdoor toilet, tin bath and mangle are reminders of life without the many household gadgets we take for granted today.

A Sparkbrook family in their front garden, *c*. 1935.

Men celebrating a wedding, *c*. 1935.

Joseph Priestley (d. 1804). He arrived in Birmingham in 1780, already famous as a scientist and philosopher. He had discovered oxygen in 1774 and written about electricity. A member of the Lunar Society, he knew Boulton and Watt, and many other leading scientists and thinkers. Although the riots of 14 to 17 July 1791 were triggered by anti-revolutionary sentiment, the rioters real motives were greed and envy. The victims were mainly Unitarians and high profile figures in local society and business. Priestley's house, his laboratory, library, scientific papers and experiments were all destroyed, and he left soon after for America.

The Larches, c. 1870. Fair Hill was eventually rebuilt and renamed the Larches. It was the last home of William Withering (d. 1799) who discovered the importance of the foxglove for treating heart disease.

Sparkbrook House, 1792. The elegant home of George Humphreys, Unitarian and merchant, was located opposite the Angel Inn and was ransacked on the third day of the riots.

Attwood Gardens, September 1975. This new public open space was created as part of the redevelopment around Larches Street. It was opened by Roy Hattersley, at the microphone, Labour Member of Parliament for Sparkbrook for 33 years.

Tree planting at Attwood Gardens, April 1980. The statue of Thomas Attwood was moved from Calthorpe Park to this site. Attwood (d. 1856) was one of Birmingham's first two Members of Parliament in 1838, and founder of the Birmingham Political Union. He lived at the Larches 1807 to 1811.

Christ Church, Grantham Road, c. 1870. It was largely paid for by the Lloyd family and was consecrated in 1867. Less than twenty years later, this splendid view was cluttered by new houses. The spire was demolished in 1918 and the tower was squared off at the arches after bomb damage in 1940.

Grantham Road, c. 1910.

Farm, Sampson Road, 1932. This graceful Georgian house was built from 1758 for Sampson Lloyd II (d. 1807), miller and ironmaster. In 1765 he was co-founder, with John Taylor of nearby Bordesley Hall, of the banking business known today as Lloyds TSB. The Lloyds were Quakers and early employees had to promise not to play cards or haunt taverns! In 1791, Sampson Lloyd, 'with soft words and refreshments' persuaded the rioters not to damage Farm. His daughter-in-law Rebecca (d. 1854), who also lived here, was a leading campaigner against slavery.

Owen's Farm, 1932. This was the old farmhouse purchased by Sampson Lloyd in 1745, with fifty-six acres of land on which Farm was to be built.

Stables and outbuildings at Farm, with the newly built Christ Church in the distance, c. 1870. Many local road names commemorate the Lloyd connection with Sparkbrook: Dolobran, Montgomery, Dearman, Braithwaite as well as Lloyd, Sampson and Farm.

Farm Park, 1968. In 1919, the Lloyd family left Farm, the family home for five generations. The house and land were donated to the city by Alderman John Henry Lloyd for recreational use.

Play fort and mound, 1968. An elaborate and rather risky adventure playground was opened that year.

Aerial wire, 1968. The gift of 1919 included the house, outbuildings, gardens, paddocks, pool, ice-age boulder and nine acres of land. Most of the original fifty-six acres of the estate had already been sold off for housing.

The slides, 1968. It was some years before Farm was used as a public park. It was initially leased to the BSA for recreation, and in the 1920s its sports days and flower shows were held here.

Anderton's Farm, 1890. Also known as Green Style farm, it was worked by several generations of Andertons. The farm land was sold off from the 1870s, and the house itself was demolished by 1900.

View down Anderton Road from the canal bridge, 1954. Behind the hedge on the left is the Sydenham Hotel. The towered building in the middle distance is the Marlborough public house. This area is being extensively redeveloped and the Marlborough is virtually the only old building still standing.